There is an enormous variety of design in corn dollies. This shows a comparatively simple design executed to perfection by the late Mr Alec Coker of Chalgrove, Oxfordshire.

STRAW AND STRAW CRAFTSMEN

Arthur Staniforth

Shire Publications Ltd

CONTENTS

Printed in Great Britain by C. I. Thomas & Sons (Haverfordwest) Ltd, Press Buildings, Merlins Bridge, Haverfordwest, Dyfed SA61 1XF.

ACKNOWLEDGEMENTS

The author expresses his thanks to the many people who have helped him with information for this book and who have in many cases provided photographs or allowed him to take photographs. These include the following: Mr. J. Brackenbury of Thame; Mrs M. Bradbury of Much Cowarne, Herefordshire; Mr A. Coker of Charlgrove, Oxford; M. E. Charbonneau of Vitry le Francois, Marne; Mrs M. E. Crawley of Clanfield, Oxford; Mr T. Dodd of Boxford, Newbury; Messrs M. W. Egerton of Gomshall, Guildford; Mr J. G. Gwynne of Dudley; Mr J. F. Hawkins of Pitstone Green Farm, Ivinghoe; Mr George Hawthorne of the Berkshire College of Agriculture; Mr and Mrs Ingleson, Streatley, Berkshire; Mr J. Leverett of Filkins, Lechlade; M. R. Mitteau of Bazancourt, Marne; Mrs F. Rudman of Goosey, Faringdon; Mr R. H. Towers, Orkney; Mr F. Tustin of Great Tew, Oxford; Mrs M. Nicholls of Luton Museum; Mr G. A. Wright of Somerton, Somerset; Mr K. Fedorowicz of Oxford.

Illustrations are acknowledged as follows: Mr A. Coker, page 1; Mr T. Dodd, pages 9 (bottom), 11; Ministry of Agriculture, Fisheries and Food, Crown Copyright, pages 9 (top), 14 (all), 15 (both), 16 (top—by courtesy of Mr J. H. Hawkins), 16 (bottom), 17, 19 (both), 20 (bottom two), 23 (bottom), 24, 25 (top), 26, 30, 31 (bottom right); Museum of English Rural Life, University of Reading, pages 3, 4; Oxford Mail and Times, pages 8 (bottom), 21; Mrs F. Rudman, page 7 (right); Mr R. H. Towers, page 29.

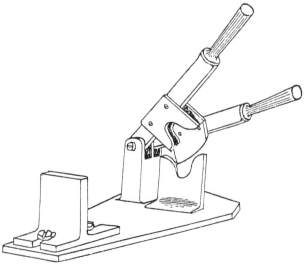

RIGHT: *A hand-operated header and trimmer for straw envelopes (from the Journal of the Ministry of Agriculture, July 1923). The operation consisted of squeezing tight the loose, unsewn end of the envelope, binding it and clipping off any surplus straw by means of the guillotine. The pallet is adjustable to accommodate different lengths of envelopes.*

COVER: *Mr George Hawthorne, lately of the Berkshire College of Agriculture, demonstrating the making of bee skeps from wheat straw.*

Traditional harvesting with horse and binder.

INTRODUCTION

Straw, which makes up about half of the total dry matter yield of cereal crops, was once a greatly valued by-product of the harvest. Now, over much of the corn-growing world, it is simply dropped on the ground behind the combine harvester and is regarded as an embarrassment by the farmer. This change in attitude may be traced to the advent of cheap petroleum, which has revolutionised farming since the 1940s. With the recent steep increases in oil prices, it is interesting to look back on some of the uses to which straw was put in the past. Some of the old uses have not yet died out and there may be scope for some of them to return in today's changing circumstances.

The most important uses for straw for centuries were in feeding and bedding livestock. In many arable areas cattle were kept during the winter as much for the production of farmyard manure as for meat. All the straw was traditionally hand-forked from field to stack, from stack to stockyard, from yard to dunghill and thence back to the land. In some districts

3

as much pride was taken in the building of dunghills as in the making of corn stacks. It was even considered by many farmers to be an advantage to turn dunghills at least once in order to ensure good fermentation and the production of short, friable manure. Some yarded cattle, particularly those being 'stored' for later fattening, would also be fed large quantities of straw. Even with the decline of mixed farming in the cereal-growing areas, these two uses remain the most important, accounting for perhaps one half of straw production in the United Kingdom. However, we shall not be considering these uses for straw in detail in this book, but concentrating on what might be called craft uses for straw.

The purposes to which straw has been put in the past are myriad. From the earliest times it has been used for bedding for humans as well as animals. A depth of clean, fresh straw does indeed make a pleasant bed, as anyone will recall who has lain upon the fragrant, springy wheat straw of a freshly opened stack. Straw mattresses or palliasses were in very common use until recent times in Britain and many will remember the three square 'biscuits' or thin

palliasses that formed the soldier's bed in barracks during the Second World War. Straw is remarkably resistant to compression and has been used from time immemorial to provide buffers between ships and the quay, or stuffing for horse collars, or, more recently, as barriers on race tracks, or for other like purposes. There are endless ways, too, in which straw has been used for decoration, from embellishments for thatch to wall coverings and straw pictures, or the lining of trinket boxes and delicate marquetry. Straw has been used for centuries to make bricks or to mix with clay to make cob or, nowadays, to mix with concrete for certain purposes. Straw is widely used in many parts of the world for mushroom growing or to provide a bed in cucumber houses and for many other horticultural purposes.

It has been possible in this book to deal with only a selection of the more interesting examples of straw use. For information about other uses, and for more detailed treatment of some purposes that are dealt with in this book, readers are invited to consult the bibliography at the end of the text.

Threshing before the advent of the combine harvester. The straw was elevated from the threshing drum to the straw stack.

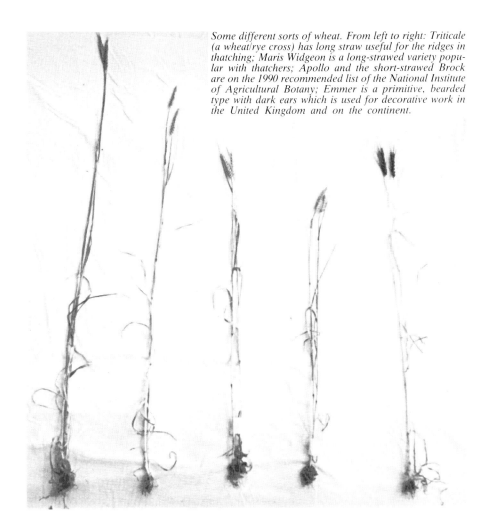

Some different sorts of wheat. From left to right: Triticale (a wheat/rye cross) has long straw useful for the ridges in thatching; Maris Widgeon is a long-strawed variety popular with thatchers; Apollo and the short-strawed Brock are on the 1990 recommended list of the National Institute of Agricultural Botany; Emmer is a primitive, bearded type with dark ears which is used for decorative work in the United Kingdom and on the continent.

STRAW – THE RAW MATERIAL

The quality of straw and its suitability for particular purposes may be affected by a number of circumstances. The type of crop, whether wheat, rye, oats or barley, or even the variety within the type, may be important. Cultivation or harvesting methods may also affect the nature of the straw.

TYPE OF CEREAL

Rye is generally the tallest of the cereals grown in temperate countries and the older varieties were often 1.5 metres (5 feet) in length. Wheat, oats and barley usually have shorter straw. The length is important for certain purposes: thatchers need a length of between 700 and 900 millimetres (28-35 inches) or more, as well as other qualities, in their straw. For ropemaking long rye straw is considered the best. Barley usually has a comparatively soft and supple straw, while wheat straw is often stiff and hard. This means that barley

5

straw may be particularly suitable for stuffing fabrics while, on the other hand, the stiffness of wheat straw makes it suitable for thatching. The awns of barley straw are tenacious, harsh and uncomfortable to the touch and rule it out for some purposes. The short, lax nature of barley straw also makes it unsuitable for thatch.

VARIETIES

Modern commonly cultivated wheat varieties may vary in straw length from 700 to 900 millimetres (28-35 inches). Older sorts of wheat were often much longer in the straw and a variety such as Yeoman may have a top internode or *pipe* as long as the total straw length of a modern semi-dwarf such as Brock. A long top internode is particularly valuable for some crafts. Some spring wheats have the slim pipes with little taper that are required for fine corn dolly work. On the other hand, the thick lower internodes of some of the winter oat varieties may be best suited to marquetry work. The straw of wheat varieties differs in that some sorts have completely hollow stems (as do normally those of the other main slender-stemmed cereals), but some have pith-filled internodes and some are intermediate. The so called solid-stemmed varieties are unsuited to some straw crafts. Cereal varieties also differ in straw colour and in wheat the colour ranges from a rosy hue through a deep golden to almost white. These colour differences may be important for some of the decorative uses of straw.

METHOD OF CULTIVATION

The amount of fertiliser that is applied to the cereal crop may affect the length and quality of its straw. Thus heavy dressings of nitrogen may lead to longer straw, which may lean over or 'lodge'. Insufficient potash and plentiful nitrogen may lead to a weak straw or one that is readily attacked by moulds. Growth-regulating chemicals are often applied to cereals in Europe today and they tend to make the straw shorter and thicker. The sowing rate of the crop may also affect the nature of the straw. Thus, in Tuscany, when wheat was specially grown there for making straw plait in the nineteenth century, it was the custom to sow thickly so as to obtain a tall, attenuated stem.

HARVESTING AND THRESHING

The stage of maturity at which the crop is cut has an important effect on the straw. In general, the earlier the crop is cut the more undamaged and durable will be the straw. For ropemaking rye was commonly cut before the grain had formed and rye cut at this early stage is also sometimes used for thatching. For the best wheat straw for thatching the crop should be cut by binder when the nodes, or 'knees', are still green and the heads erect; the crop will ripen further in stook and stack and give the full yield of grain as well as a durable thatching straw. If a cereal crop is harvested late the straw tends to become brittle and may be infected by fungi; it may lose some of its wax content and its brightness and will become less suitable for many purposes.

For corn dolly making it is normally essential to harvest straw complete with ears that are not so ripe as to 'shatter' with handling. Small plots of suitable varieties may be grown for this purpose and small stocks of their seed are still maintained in Britain. Such plots may be cut by sickle or scythe and sheaves of corn cut at a suitable stage by binder may also be used for corn dollies. For thatching, or whenever a long, undamaged straw is required, it is best to harvest by binder and to cut with as short a stubble as possible. For the high quality thatching straw known as wheat 'reed' the sheaves from the binder, after stooking and stacking, are threshed in a special machine known as a reed comber, which beats only the ears of the corn. These machines carry the straw forward horizontally, comb out the loose leaves, weeds and short straws and then tie the combed straw in bundles, or *nitches*, ready for the thatcher or other craftsman. A few combine harvesters have been adapted to thresh and comb in a similar manner.

For straw plait the wheat was carefully cut so as to avoid damaging the pipe and individual stems were drawn out so as to detach as much leaf and leaf sheath as possible and then gathered into special sheaves, which were bound just below the ears. The ears were then cut off, to be separately threshed for the grain, leaving the undamaged straw to be cut up and split for plaiting.

The requirements for straw for the once important craft of horse collar making were

Cutting wheat with a fagging hook (left) and with a scythe (right).

set out in the *Journal of the Board of Agriculture,* Volume XVII for May 1910. Horse collars needed to be stuffed with long, tough straw and the bigger collars needed straw at least 1.5 metres (5 feet) long. Both wheat and rye straw were tough enough, but only the longest rye straw was suitable for the bigger collars. The 1910 journal mentions one firm which used about 150 tons of home-grown rye straw each year but which was even then finding it 'increasingly difficult to obtain straw suitable for the purpose'. A great deal of foreign rye straw had to be imported. The journal describes how the straw was prepared. It was often threshed by hand and was then 'combed in a very simple way, frequently by hand, or with a very short-handled rake, which is passed through the butt end of the sheaf; or the sheaf may be taken with both hands and

pulled several times through a row of wooden prongs which, pointing upwards, are firmly fixed to a trestle about four feet in height'.

The modern combine harvester treats the crop quite roughly as it goes through the threshing drum and the straw is left in a swath on the ground. When picked up by the conventional small square baler this straw is subjected to a ramming, chopping action that will make it unsuitable for any craft requiring long, unbroken straw. However, the big round balers that are now commonly used collect the straw with a much kinder action and, provided it has the necessary length and other qualities, straw from these round bales can be satisfactory for certain purposes such as the making of archery targets.

It is essential for all craftsmen and manufacturers working with straw to be

clear about the quality and quantity that they are likely to require and then to make suitable arrangements with growers in good time for the production of such straw. Provided that they have a reliable market, corn growers, particularly on the smaller farms, can still be found who will supply straw to suit a variety of needs. But too often the straw user neglects to organise his supply in advance and is left hunting for his raw material after the harvest is over so that he has to take what quality he can find.

TOP: *Maris Huntsman wheat — straw length about 900 mm (35 inches) — being stooked to ripen before stacking and later threshing and combing for thatch. Note the erect ears. Photograph taken at Mr M. Drew's Middle Farm, Hailey, near Witney, in 1980.*

LEFT: *Feeding sheaves into the reed comber. Photographed at Captain C. R. Radclyffe's farm at Lew, Oxford.*

ABOVE: *A load of bundles, or 'nitches', of wheat reed coming off the comber. The reed amounts to about half the total weight of the straw. Note the chaff being blown into a sheeted trailer and baled combings on the trailer at the rear. Photograph taken at Mr G. Cox's Lovells Court Farm, Hinton Waldrist, Oxfordshire, in 1980.*

BELOW: *Mr T. Dodd of Combesbury Farm, Boxford, Newbury, cutting a crop of rye just before the seed is set. After drying and bleaching in the stook such straw can be used for thatching and is ideal for certain crafts. A second crop can be taken from the land after removal of the rye.*

Peaks of perfection in the stack thatcher's craft. Mr John Scoley of White House Farm, Whisby, Lincoln, won the Metheringham Agricultural Society's thatching competition in 1953 with this work. A few years later the combine harvester had taken over from the binder and such stackyards became only a memory.

THATCHING

Until combine harvesters took over from binders in the 1950s it was usual for corn farmers in Britain to reserve at least one stack of good, clean wheat straw for thatching the next season's corn and hay stacks. This was straw that had been through the threshing drum and elevated, loose, on to the straw stack.

It was important, at hay and corn harvest, to build stacks with a good roof with a steep pitch and no hollows and men who could do this were among the most important craftsmen on the farm. After the stack had settled, it was normally thatched. A wagon load of wheat straw would be drawn up alongside and shaken out into a circular pile. The water cart would be filled at the pond and pulled beside the pile and buckets full of water would be thrown over the loose straw until it was thoroughly wetted. The straw was then drawn out from the bottom of the pile, using both hands, usually by the thatcher's mate, who shuff-led backwards, leaving a band of straight straws across the face of the pile. The drawn straw was then gathered or *gabbled* — to use the East Anglian term — into flat *yealms* about 460 millimetres (18 inches) wide and placed in a yoke. This was an elongated fork, usually cut from a hedge, which would hold perhaps ten yealms.

The thatcher, meanwhile, would be laying yealms on the roof of the stack and when his yoke was empty he would call 'Shoof'. His mate would then mount the ladder with the heavy yokeful or 'shoof' of wet gabbled straw and place it conveniently for the thatcher, before returning with the empty yoke to resume pulling straw. The thatch, when laid, would be wetted again, combed with a long thatching comb and then held down by three or four rows of twine around the stack, attached to straight thatching pegs, or *brotches* as they were known in the eastern counties, thrust into the stack horizontally.

Although some farms, particularly the larger ones, would have men able to thatch stacks, the work was commonly done by local craftsmen, who would make thatch pegs or hurdles or other types of fencing in the winter. The work of thatching stacks was hard. The moving of the long ladders was itself an art and, even with the leather knee-caps and the thimbles that thatchers habitually wore, rheumatics in the hands and knees were a hazard of the trade.

Stack thatching has now almost died out in the United Kingdom. But house thatching, though much reduced in scope since previous centuries, still prospers as a country craft, mainly in England south of a line from the Severn to the Wash. The thatching of houses and barns, and even of

Mr Edward Hutchins thatching a barn near Newbury, Berkshire, with whole sheaves of rye straw.

a few churches and some public buildings, is sometimes done with long straw, prepared in a manner similar to that used for stack thatching. But more commonly today *combed wheat reed* is used. This 'reed', specially prepared so as to resemble the true Norfolk reed, is supplied in bundles, or nitches, ready for placing on the roof to be thatched. Thatching with combed wheat reed gives a neater appearance than does the long straw method. It also tends to last longer than long straw, though not as long as the true Norfolk reed.

Rye straw is also occasionally used for thatching. One system is to cut the rye crop with a binder before the grain has fully formed and to use the whole sheaves, un-threshed and uncombed, for thatching. A very good yield of straw per acre is thus obtained and the considerable expense of threshing and combing is avoided. However, the final appearance of the roof is not as neat as with wheat reed and it cannot be expected to last as long.

It is estimated that there are still some fifty thousand thatched houses in England and there are about five hundred thatching businesses, almost all small family firms, to keep them in good order. The thatched house, cottage or inn has an established place in popular esteem and the planning authorities usually encourage the maintenance of thatch as a roofing material where it already exists. It seems likely that a steady demand for the thatcher's craft will continue for many years. Thatchers are quite well paid for their work and there is a good demand for apprenticeships with master thatchers. The Rural Development Commission (formerly CoSIRA) sponsors regular training courses for thatchers and many experts consider that the general standard of thatching in Britain has never been higher than it is today.

THATCH FINIALS

A country craft allied to thatching is the making of ornaments, usually in the form of birds or animals, to be placed on the ridges of thatched buildings.

The finials may be fashioned in different ways. Straw birds can be made by carefully folding and shaping a bundle of straw and then tying up the tail and the head and neck with binder twine. However, a more durable ornament is made by using wire netting. The body of the bird or animal is built around a central core or frame of suitable material, such as wire, and is then covered with wire netting, drawn tightly around it so that it retains its shape. Hazel pegs are firmly inserted to serve both as legs and as a secure attachment to the thatched roof. These ornaments do not last many years. However, it is usual to renew the ridge of thatched buildings every ten years or so and this provides an opportunity to replace the straw cockerel, pheasant, owl or fox, as the case may be.

It is not possible to discern any consistent local preferences for particular finials. It is often the particular ability of a local thatcher, who is good at, say, peacocks or geese, that sets the fashion in a district. But one or two craftsmen are now specialising in making these finials and export their work to thatchers in widely separated areas.

LIP WORK

In the nineteenth century the craft of lip work was widespread in the United Kingdom. Well prepared straw was passed through a short length of cow horn, about 30 millimetres ($1\frac{1}{8}$ inches) in diameter, to form an untwisted continuous roll, which was coiled and bound together by split bramble cut in winter before the rise of sap, or other suitable material, to form circular containers such as bushel skeps or baskets or beehives. In south-east England it was common for farmworkers to make their own beehives from straw provided by the farmer. It was an inefficient method of keeping bees as the swarm was lost when the honey was taken and these primitive hives quickly disappeared when modern sectional wooden hives came into general use.

However, straw bee skeps are still re-

ABOVE: *Mr G. A. Wright of Somerton, Somerset, a former thatcher, making straw finials.* BELOW: *A Bunyard fruit store (left) at Little Orchard, Streatley, Berkshire. These stores, designed by a Kentish horticulturalist, George Bunyard (1841-1919), were insulated by straw thatch and the walls were constructed of a 6 inch (150 mm) layer of packed straw. One is still used as an apple store at the Chilton Estate, Chilton Foliat.*

quired today by beekeepers, but only for the collection of swarms. The craft is not dead and is still taught by bee instructors at one or two British county colleges. Long, clean straw — preferably of rye or wheat — is required. Hand cutting and threshing will provide small quantities of suitable straw but wheat reed produced in the manner described earlier is also good for this craft. Lip work is still an important country craft in some parts of Europe and large numbers of baskets made in this manner are imported into Britain from countries such as Poland. In Holland, moreover, bees are still kept in straw hives, some in large commercial apiaries with suitably adapted management.

THIS PAGE AND OPPOSITE: *Mr George Hawthorne demonstrates the making of bee skeps from wheat straw. Note the use of a length of cow horn to keep the layers tight and even. The home-made hollow awl allows the binding — split cane in this case — to be threaded through the lower layer.*

ABOVE: *Bee skeps of late Victorian date from Pitstone Green Farm Museum, near Ivinghoe, Buckinghamshire.*

LEFT: *A modern clothes basket of lip work made from rye straw and imported from Poland.*

Equipment used in the straw plait industry. One method of splitting straw was to pass it through the apertures in small instruments such as those shown here. The roller, which was often attached to the cottage door post, was used to flatten and soften the strips.

STRAW PLAIT

Straw plait was originally made from whole straws but, as stated in an article in the *Illustrated London News* of November 1878, 'it was in the eighteenth century, by the ingenuity of some French prisoners of war' that a tool for the splitting of straw came into use. These tools consisted of orifices with a variable number of vanes in them through which the straw was passed in order to split it into from three to ten fine slivers. These would then be rolled between wooden rollers to take out the stiffness and then plaited into ribbons, some of great fineness. There was a very great demand for straw hats and a large trade grew up. William Cobbett strongly supported the craft. James Caird, writing on *British Agriculture* in 1852, reported: 'Locally grown wheat straw of special quality went for plaiting at Dunstable . . . as valuable by

the acre as corn.' The *Illustrated London News* wrote that 'the plaiting work some years ago was mostly done by little children in the "plait schools" kept by a class of old women in the villages around Luton, whose occupation has been stopped by the Education Act of 1870. An expert woman can make 40 yards of straw plait in a day of 12 hours but will earn only 7s 6d a week, yet in a busy season there are those who come from London to Luton or Dunstable for temporary employment.' This article describes country folk who 'plait as they sit at their cottage doors in the summer or at their firesides in winter, as they walk round the village street, tend sheep on the hillsides, or pay a visit to the market town'.

The plait was used for a variety of purposes but the most important one was for hatmaking. The plait was sewn into the desired shape of hat or bonnet. This was then stiffened by being passed through a solution of gelatin and dried, and then it was shaped in a press. Even by 1878 the *Illustrated London News* reported: 'Straw plait has of late years suffered greatly from the competition of Canton or Chinese plait.' The *Encyclopaedia Britannica* of 1911 noted that 'the plaiting of straw . . . formerly gave employment to many thousands of women and young children; but now vast quantities of plaits are imported at a very cheap rate from Italy, China and Japan.' Straw plaiting died out in England soon after the First World War and all that is now left of a once large industry are a few old hats, some remnants of plait and a few old tools of the trade in museums in eastern England. However, there is still one factory in Luton which makes hats from straw plait, using the same machinery as in former times, but only imported plait.

LEFT: *The 'Illustrated London News' of 1878 included this picture of girls plaiting straw by lamplight.*

RIGHT: *How the plait was sewn into bonnets — from the 'Illustrated London News' of 1878.*

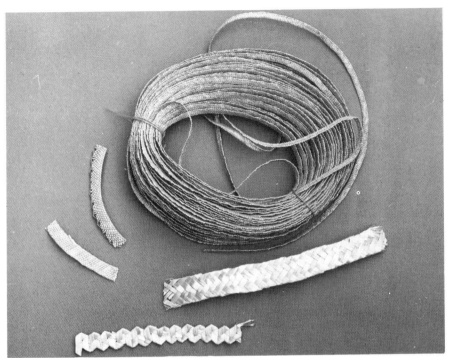

ABOVE: *There were many scores of designs of straw plait — these are only a few from the Pitstone Green Farm Museum. Two are made from flattened whole straw, the others from split straw.*

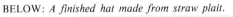

BELOW: *A finished hat made from straw plait.*

TOP: *Making straw rope at a farm near Beaconsfield, Buckinghamshire, in the early years of the twentieth century. The lengths of rope, seen twisted upon themselves, were used to bind up bundles of straw coming from the threshing drum for later transport to London.*

ABOVE: *A sample of half-inch (13 mm) diameter straw rope made from oat straw. Note the nylon thread reinforcement.*

LEFT: *A selection of whimbles at Asthall Barrow Farm Museum, near Burford, Oxfordshire.*

20

Making straw rope at Clanfield Mill, Witney, Oxfordshire, in the early 1970s. The machines have been moved and now work at a factory at Dudley, West Midlands.

STRAW ROPE

The line between true handicrafts and small-scale industry is not always clear. The making of straw plait into hats was a considerable industry based upon craft skills. A number of other uses of straw fall into the category of rural industry.

Straw rope was used by thatchers to hold down thatch; similar rope was also used to tie bales of hay or straw which were cut from the stack by a hay knife. A simple tool known as a *whimmer* or *whimble*, consisting of a hook on a crank, was used and two operators were needed. One would engage the hook in long supple straw from a heap or stack and start twisting the crank. He would move backwards, continually twisting, while his partner, using a leather pad to protect the hand that held the twisting straw, fed more straw from the heap, evenly, on to the end of the rope as it formed. The method was very simple but it

required practice to make rope of even thickness and strength.

At one time straw rope of this type was required in great quantities for packing goods of many types and for use in iron foundries, and machines were designed to spin it in various thicknesses. Long, strong and supple straw was needed and rye cut before the grain had formed was considered ideal. The straw was fed by operators into two troughs from which it was led to spinners; the two strands were then spun into one rope, which was passed on to a winding drum. Such machines could make rope which varied in thickness from about 12 to 50 millimetres ($\frac{1}{2}$ inch to 2 inches).

The *Journal of the Ministry of Agriculture and Fisheries* in 1923 said that straw rope was 'an article of extensive and extending use' and suggested that imports could be saved if more were made on British farms. However, alternative packing materials were developed, particularly when the petrochemical industry expanded, and there now remains only one straw rope factory in operation in Britain. Straw rope making requires considerable hand labour and skill and this has driven up the costs. It also needs a reliable supply of suitable straw, which has proved difficult to ensure. In recent years, as strong rye straw became scarce, it has been customary to include a strand of nylon thread in the rope to give it the necessary strength and this, too, has increased costs.

A somewhat similar straw-based pack-ing material, known as Polypaille, is made in France. The straw is made into thin mats between black plastic sheets. Conventional bales of straw are fed into a coarse chopper and the chopped straw is blown into a hopper from which it is drawn out by toothed rollers on to a moving belt between sheets of light gauge plastic, which are stuck together at the edges and stitched together across the width of the mat by thin thread. The mats vary between 100 millimetres (4 inches) and 2 metres (6$\frac{1}{2}$ feet) in width and they are rolled off on a spindle for dispatch. Barley straw is always used as other straws puncture the plastic.

ARCHERY TARGETS

Archery targets were made in some country districts at least up to the Second World War by forming heavy gauge straw rope into coils and sewing it tightly together. This process has now been partially mechanised at a factory near Guildford in Surrey. Long, tough straw, preferably of rye or oats, is tightly compressed to form a thick rope, which is rectangular in section. This is coiled and stitched together with strong nylon thread. The targets are made in small, medium and full sizes and covered for use with the necessary ringed paper. Straw collected in big round bales behind the combine harvester is suitable for processing in this way. The Egerton factory at Gomshall has become well known for this craft and has supplied targets for the Olympic Games. Such targets are reputed to be able to withstand the impact of up to two hundred thousand arrows, under average conditions, before disintegrating.

STRAW MATS

A machine was designed in Victorian times to stitch straw together to make a mat which could be used for thatching or for sheep folds or similar purposes. This machine consisted of a feed table from which straw was passed by means of a sprocket wheel to the stitching device. This made two parallel rows of stitches, some 180 millimetres (7 inches) apart, with binder twine. The straw emerged from the machine as a continuous mat, whose thickness and evenness depended mainly upon the rate of feed.

The original Victorian machine was hand-driven but an improved version, driven by a small oil engine and called the Spider thatch-making machine, was brought out at the beginning of the Second World War. In the West of England, in particular, there was a great expansion of corn growing and few skilled thatchers were available to cover the stacks after harvest. The Spider machine was intended to make good the shortage of craftsmen. The author operated one of these thatch-making machines at the Somerset County Farm Institute at Cannington in 1941. It took time and practice to feed the straw accurately and evenly and we rarely if ever achieved the target of 450 metres (500 yards) of mat per day. Combed wheat reed is the best straw to use in a Spider machine, but we often had to deal with straw that was tangled or partly mixed with docks or thistles. Machine-made thatching mats were usually cut in lengths of 3 to 3.7 metres (10 to 12 feet), which were pegged down on the roof of the stack so that they overlapped. The method served its purpose but the results were never as good as those

ABOVE: *Polypaille packing material made by Ets Charbonneau, near Vienne, eighty miles east of Paris.*
BELOW: *An archery target made from oat straw by the Egerton firm at Gomshall, near Guildford, Surrey.*

from real thatch put on by craftsmen.

A number of thatch-making machines can still be found on farms and in farm museums in Britain but they are now very seldom used. In Europe similar machines have been used to make mats mainly for horticultural purposes, but their use seems to have died out except in some Mediterranean areas.

One type of mat is, however, still made near Rheims in France and is widely used for displaying some kinds of cheese in shops and supermarkets. These mats are made on machines that are essentially scaled-down versions of thatch-making machines.

STRAW ENVELOPES FOR BOTTLES

At one time straw envelopes were very widely used throughout Europe to cover glass bottles to prevent breakage during transport. Britain imported, mainly from Holland and France, about 150 million envelopes in 1913. The trade fell off after the First World War but the Rural Industries Intelligence Bureau was still calling for more home production of envelopes in the *Journal of the Ministry of Agriculture* in 1923. These envelopes were still being made as recently as 1966 at Clanfield, near Witney in Oxfordshire, but the machines are now lying disused at a site in the Midlands.

The July 1923 issue of the *Journal* describes how the envelopes were made. Long, combed straw was placed in a thin, even layer in a trough alongside the stitching machine and was then doubled over upon itself before being sewn together with fine, hemp twine. The folded-over end of the straw formed the open bottom of the envelope. Two or three rows of stitches were made, according to the type of machine. At one time the envelopes were first sewn as flat mats, rather similar to those for displaying cheeses, and bent round to a circular shape and stitched together by hand. But later machines were designed to produce the envelopes in the circular form required. Some machines could be worked by treadle, but the more advanced machines, which were said to have a designed output of between two hundred and five hundred envelopes per hour, were driven by engines. After seaming, the envelopes were 'headed' by a device operated by hand or treadle.

An envelope for a quart bottle needed to be about 380 millimetres (15 inches) long, so that really long straw, more than 760 millimetres (30 inches) in length, was required. Rye straw was particularly suitable, though long, supple wheat straw was also used. Straw envelopes have now been almost entirely superseded by other forms of packing for bottles, such as corrugated paper and cardboard. The manufacture of straw envelopes is reported to have died out in the United Kingdom and in France. However, some of the vintage port that is imported into Britain is still sold in bottles protected by straw envelopes, indicating that a remnant of this once thriving local industry still survives in Europe.

Only a few bottles are today protected by straw envelopes such as this. Formerly such envelopes were made in vast numbers.

ABOVE: *Mr John Leverett demonstrates the making of straw matting on a 'Spider' machine, using wheat reed.*

BELOW: *Mats made by Ets Mitteau at Bazancourt, near Rheims, are widely used throughout France — as at this supermarket near Dunkirk — for displaying cheeses. Some are imported into Britain and are occasionally used under cheeses in grocers' shops. Wheat straw is commonly used for this purpose.*

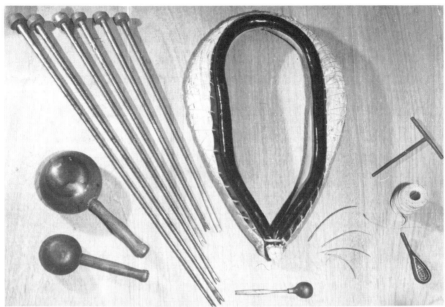

Tools of the long straw filler and a filled light van horse collar. The longest stuffing irons were used to fill the tubular forewale, the rim against which the hames fitted. The mallets of lignum vitae or metal were used to shape the contours of the collar. Half-moon needles were used to stitch together the filled body of the collar and the T-shaped twisting iron to draw the stitches tightly together.

HORSE COLLARS

At the beginning of the twentieth century there were about one million working horses on British farms and great numbers of other cart and carriage horses. At the end of the Second World War there were still half a million working horses on farms but within twenty years they had all but disappeared from the scene. Most draught horses required collars and straw was universally used to pack them. Among the thousands of skilled harness makers who were employed in those times there was a distinct class, known as long straw fillers, who specialised in packing straw into horse collars. They received the leather collars from the saddlers and filled and shaped the forewales, or rims, against which the hames were set, and also the main body of the collars. Long rye straw was preferred, though good wheat straw could be used; some was imported but some was pulled in bundles from stacks. It was usual to dampen the straw, as well as the leather work, to remove unwanted stiffness. Special rounded mallets were used to

mould the collars to the correct shape; half-moon needles were used, with Italian hemp twine, to stitch the bodywork together and twisting tools, sometimes known as Spanish winches, were employed to draw this stitching very tightly together. It was strenuous work and a skilled long straw filler could complete his task on perhaps three large carthorse collars in a day's work. When filled, the collars were sent back to the saddlers for them to sew in the checked linings and complete the caps and furnishings.

Today in Britain there are hardly any heavy horses on farms and there are only a few left pulling vehicles such as brewers' drays. But a band of enthusiasts for draught horses of all types maintains a small but steady demand for collars. Artificial packing materials have been used as substitutes for straw but connoisseurs insist they they do not equal the natural material and a few long straw fillers are still plying their traditional craft.

Mr Jack Brackenbury, of Thame, Oxfordshire, who learned the craft as a young man, demonstrates how long straw was packed into the leather collars.

An ancient cob wall at Crediton, Devon — one of many to be found in the West Country. A good coping is essential — in this case it is of thatch.

COB

There is a long tradition of using straw to bind clay and similar building materials. In England this tradition was strongest in the West Country, where 'cob' walls are still common, either free-standing or in buildings. Provided these walls are on firm, dry foundations, are properly constructed and are roofed over to prevent water getting into them, they will last for many years. Cob houses of Elizabethan date are not uncommon in Devon.

Various recipes for cob have been given. One said that 'eight bundles of barley straw, equal to one packhorse load, were mixed and tempered with nine cart loads of clay'. Another, from Wiltshire, where crushed chalk replaced the clay of Devon, said that for a 'cubic yard, throw in a double handful of short wheat straw as a binding element, and then turn with a shovel three times'. In Devon the clay and straw were often trodden together by oxen. In the construction of traditional cob walls no formers were used but the cob was pitched on, course by course, and later pared down to give a good surface. It was important to let it dry thoroughly as it was

built up. Unlike fired clay bricks, cob required no fuel in its preparation. But the craft is now virtually lost in England. Cob walls were still being made at the beginning of the twentieth century and experimental cottages were built at Amesbury in Wiltshire in 1919 to test the method: some survive, in excellent condition.

Well kept thatched cob houses, with their rounded contours and slightly irregular geometry, look delightful in their West Country setting. Those who live in them may complain that the unevenness of the walls can make it difficult to accommodate furniture or to attach shelves or hanging cupboards, or that the windows are small. Yet they will praise the excellent insulation of cob and thatch against extremes of temperature and noise. From time to time there are suggestions that this ancient form of construction should be revived and in Normandy, France, cob has been used in the construction of new houses. Perhaps one might start with some free-standing walls; there is nothing more attractive than a garden wall of cob with its coping of tiles or thatch.

RIGHT: *Mr Robert H. Towers, an Orkney chair maker, at work in his house at St Ola, Kirkwall, Orkney. A type of lip work is used in making the Orkney chair. The making of these chairs has become a quite important local craft industry in the Orkney Islands, from whence the straw-backed chairs are exported to many countries.*

RIGHT AND BELOW: *A tradition of delicate work with straw has survived in Switzerland and one feature of the work is the spinning of straw into thread. For this it is essential to start with long straw 'pipes' or internodes. Mrs Margaret Bradbury of Much Cowarne, Herefordshire, is using 20 inch 'pipes' of the old wheat variety Squareheads Master. These are split into six slivers and two of these, after moistening, are spun into a thread on a special machine which was made locally. The straw lace mat was made from straw spun by Mrs Margaret Bradbury.*

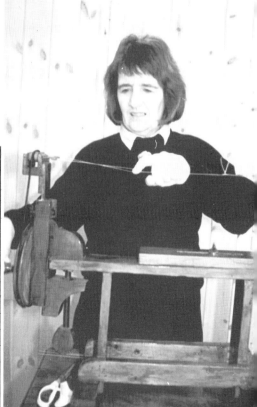

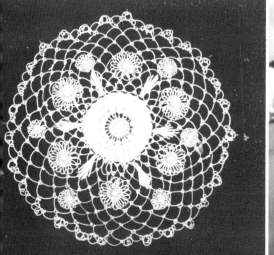

Examples of decorative work in straw.

DECORATIVE USES FOR STRAW

When harvested in good condition, straw is an attractive material. In colour it is usually a shade of gold and the silica and wax in its composition give it a brightness that is pleasing to the eye. Moreover, some types of straw have great durability. These qualities have led to its being used from very early times for decorative purposes. We have already considered straw plait and thatched roof finials but there are several other decorative uses.

Whatever may be the origins of the naking of corn dollies – in ancient fertility rites or in thanksgiving to the deity for the fruits of harvest – their main use today is as attractive decorations, made from a natural material. There has been a great vogue for corn dolly making in recent years and a number of books on the subject have been written and effectively illustrated. In a

few localities corn dolly making has even attained the status of a local industry. One West Country firm has marketed great quantities of packs of prepared straw with instructions for making dollies; another has made thousands of small dollies for display in the wrapping of food products. Making corn dollies commercially has provided useful part-time employment for women outworkers in these districts and, although their numbers cannot compare with those of the straw plaiters of the nineteenth century, they demonstrate that a handicraft of this nature can still be organised if there is a good market for the product.

There is an infinite variety of ways in which straw may be used to create pictures. There is a strong tradition for this work in the Far East and in eastern Europe but examples can be found in most cereal-growing countries and there are some skilful artists in straw in Britain. It might be thought that straw pictures and marquetry were flimsy and ephemeral but straw is durable and such work may last for centuries. There is some extraordinary work on show in Peterborough Museum, made by French prisoners of war around two hundred years ago. The Luton Museum also houses an outstanding collection of plait and other decorative straw work.

Straw is also used, particularly in the far east, as a decorative lining for sewing and trinket boxes and for boxes of all types. Straw plait is sometimes used for this purpose but, more often, graded slivers of straw are interwoven to provide an attractive pattern. Many examples can be seen in curio and craft shops, often at an astonishingly low price for items which have required great patience and dexterity in their fabrication.

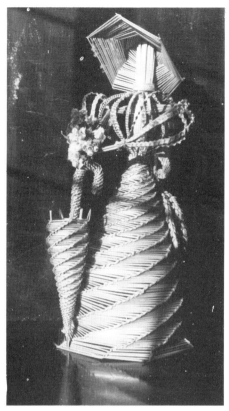

RIGHT: *A corn dolly exhibited at the 1980 Bath and West Agricultural Show by Mr and Mrs C. D. King of Bagley, Wedmore, Somerset.*
BELOW LEFT: *A picture of Durham Cathedral made from straw by Mrs Freda Rudman of Goosey, near Faringdon, Oxfordshire.*
BELOW RIGHT: *A straw picture from Poland.*

PLACES TO VISIT
Almonry Museum, Abbey Gate, Vine Street, Evesham, Worcestershire WR11 4BG. Telephone: 0386 446944
Bewdley Museum, The Shambles, Load Street, Bewdley, Worcestershire DY12 2AE. Telephone: 0299 403573.
Buckinghamshire County Museum, Church Street, Aylesbury, Buckinghamshire HP20 2QP. Telephone: 0296 88849.
Cogges Farm Museum, Church Lane, Cogges, Witney, Oxfordshire OX8 6LA. Telephone: 0993 772602.
Easton Farm Park, Easton, Woodbridge, Suffolk IP13 0EQ. Telephone: 0728 746475.
Luton Museum and Art Gallery, Wardown Park, Luton, Bedfordshire LU2 7HA. Telephone: 0582 36941.
Moonsmill Craft Museum and Gallery, 47 Cann Bridge Street, Higher Walton, Preston, Lancashire. Telephone: 0772 628036.
Museum of English Rural Life, The University, Whiteknights, Reading, Berkshire RG6 2AG. Telephone: 0734 318660.
Norfolk Rural Life Museum, Beech House, Gressenhall, East Dereham, Norfolk NR20 4DR. Telephone: 0362 860563.
Oxfordshire County Museum, Fletcher's House, Woodstock, Oxfordshire OX7 1SN. Telephone: 0993 811456.
Peterborough City Museum and Art Gallery, Priestgate, Peterborough, Cambridgeshire PE1 1LF. Telephone: 0733 43329.
Pitstone Local History Society, c/o Mrs Jeannette Wallis, Hazel Bank, Groomsby, Ivinghoe, Leighton Buzzard, Bedfordshire. Telephone: 0296 661997.
Rutland County Museum, Catmos Street, Oakham, Rutland, Leicestershire LE15 6HW. Telephone: 0572 723654.
Somerset Rural Life Museum, Abbey Farm, Chilkwell Street, Glastonbury, Somerset BA6 8DB. Telephone: 0458 32903.
Upminster Tithe Barn Agricultural and Folk Museum, Hall Lane, Upminster, Essex. Telephone: 04024 47535.
Weald and Downland Open Air Museum, Singleton, near Chichester, West Sussex PO18 0EU. Telephone: 024363 348.
Welsh Folk Museum, St Fagans, Cardiff, South Glamorgan CF5 6XB. Telephone: 0222 569441.

FURTHER READING
Coker, A. *The Craft of Straw Decoration*. Dryad, 1971.
Davis, Jean. *Straw Plait*. Shire Publications Ltd, 1981.
Fearn, Jacqueline. *Thatch and Thatching*. Shire Publications Ltd, 1976.
Lambeth, M. *Discovering Corn Dollies*. Shire Publications Ltd, 1977.
McCann, John. *Clay and Cob Buildings*. Shire Publications Ltd, 1983.
Ministry of Agriculture. 'Straw ropes and straw envelopes', *Journal of the Ministry of Agriculture*, volume 30, number 4 (1923) 331-42.
Rural Industries Bureau. *The Thatcher's Craft*, 1961.
Staniforth, A. R. *Cereal Straw*. Oxford University Press, 1980.
West, Robert. *Thatch*. David and Charles, 1987.
Whitmore, R. *Of Uncommon Interest*. Spurbooks Ltd, 1975.
Williams-Ellis, C. and Eastwick-Field, E. 'Building in Cob, Pisé and Stabilised Earth'. *Country Life*, 1947.
Zimmermann, Gretl. *Straw Stars*. Search Books, 1968.

The Guild of Straw Craftsmen, established 1989, aims to extend the range and improve the quality of straw craftsmanship in the United Kingdom. The secretary of the guild is: Mrs Ella Carstairs, Conifer Cottage, Buck Brigg, Hanworth , Norfolk NR11 7HH. Telephone: 0263 761615